中小学英语
教学改革丛书

浙江大学 — 宁波镇海区外语教学改革合作项目

BILINGUAL TEACHERS'
HANDBOOK SERIES:

双语教师手册：

小学数学与科学分册

Primary Mathematics and Science

主　编　黄建滨

编　者　于书林　陈伶俐　郑照阳　宣　璐　宋丹贵

ZHEJIANG UNIVERSITY PRESS
浙江大学出版社

$\mathbf{C}$ontents 目 录

课前用语

Let's get ready for class.

准备上课。

Class begins.

上课了。

Who's on duty today?

今天谁值日?

Is everyone here?

都到齐了吗?

Who's absent today?

今天谁没来?

What day is it today?

今天是星期几?

What's the date today?

今天是几号?

I'm sorry I'm late. /Excuse me for coming late.

对不起，我迟到了。

Please come earlier next time.

下次请早点到。

Li Hong, have you collected all the exercise books?

李红，作业本都收齐了吗？

Here are your exercise books. Please hand them out.

这是你们的练习本，请发下去。

Monitor, would you please fetch some chalk for me?

班长能帮我去拿些粉笔来吗？

I'm sorry to have kept you so long.

对不起耽搁大家这么久。

Be quiet!

安静！

Silence, please.

请安静！

Stand up, please.

起立！

Sit down, please.

坐下！

Sit up well.

坐好！

One, two, three, go/start!

一、二、三, 开始!

Ready?

准备好了吗?

Quickly!

快!

Hurry up!

赶快!

课堂用语

Open your books, please.

请翻开书。

Please turn to Page 20.

请翻到书本的二十页。

Please take out your notebooks/exercise books.

请拿出笔记本/练习本。

No more talking, please.

请安静。

Attention, please.

请注意。

Let's have a dictation.

让我们来听写。

We're going to have a new lesson today.

今天我们要上新课。

First let's have a revision.

首先让我们复习一下。

Who can answer this question?

谁能回答这个问题?

Do you have any questions?

你们有问题吗?

Let me see.

让我看看/想想。

Put up your hands if you have any questions.

如果有问题请举手。

Raise your hands, please.

请举手。

Hands down.

把手放下。

Repeat after me./Follow me.

跟我读。

Listen to me, please.

请听我说。

Look at the blackboard/screen, please.

请看黑板/屏幕。

All eyes on me, please.

请都看着我。

Let's read it together. Ready, go!

大家齐声朗读, 预备, 起!

Read slowly and clearly.

读慢一点, 清楚一点。

Don't be nervous.

不要紧张。

Any one can help him/her?

谁来帮他/她一下?

Any volunteers?

有自告奋勇的吗?

I beg your pardon?

对不起, 能再说一遍吗?

Take it easy.

请放心/别紧张。

Be brave/active, please.

请勇敢/主动些。

Who wants to try?

谁想试试?

Come (up) to the front, please.

请到前面来。

Go back to your seat, please.

请回你的座位。

Come on. You can do it.

来吧! 你能做到的。

Let's play a game.

让我们玩个游戏。

Are you tired? Let's take a break.

累了吗? 我们休息一下吧。

Look up the word in the dictionary.

在词典里查这个词。

Whose turn is it?

轮到谁了?

Now you're going to read one by one.

现在你们依次朗读。

Who's next?

接下来是谁?

You're next.

接下来是你。

It's your turn.

轮到你了。

Just hands. No voices.

不要说, 请举手。

Do it on your own.

自己做。

From the very beginning.

从头开始。

Please read it to the end.

请读到结尾。

Stop here, please.

请停下来。

Hands up before you answer.

回答问题前，请举手。

That's all for today./We stop here for today.

今天就到这里。

Let's call it a day.

今天就到这里。

Class is over. Thank you, class.

下课。谢谢！

Good-bye.

再见！

See you tomorrow.

明天见！

Who wants to come to the front?

谁愿意到前面来？

Too slowly!

太慢了！

Loudly!

大声点儿!

Look at your books.

看你的书本。

Look at me/her/him.

看我/她/他。

Listen and do the action.

听并做动作。

Listen and repeat.

听并重复。

Listen and answer the question.

听然后回答问题。

Listen read and spell the words.

听读并拼出这些单词。

Listen and read twice for each word.

听并把每个词读两遍。

Read and write.

读并写。

Please write it on the blackboard.

请把它写在黑板上。

Please write the words in your exercise book.

请把这些词写在你的练习本上。

Please write these sentences on a piece of paper.

请把这些句子写在一张纸上。

Please fill in the blanks in your workbook.

请在你的活动用书上填空。

Have a try.

试一试。

Try again, please.

请再试一次。

Once more, please.

请再来一遍。

Pay more attention to this, please.

请多注意这一点。

Now please work in groups.

现在开始小组讨论。

Talk to your partner.

跟你的同桌讨论。

Tell your desk mate.

告诉你的同桌。

Can you solve this problem?

你能解决这个问题吗?

Who wants to try?

谁想试一试?

Who wants to do it on the blackboard?

谁愿意到黑板上来做?

Are you through?/Have you finished?

做完了吗?

You did a very good job.

你做得不错。

Very good. /Good try. /Well done!

完成得不错。

Terrific! /Wonderful! /Excellent!

很棒!

Please give him/her a big hand.

请给他/她一些掌声。

Can you follow me?

能跟上吗?

Do you understand?

你听懂了吗?

Come on, you're almost there.

来吧! 你快(做/答)对了。

I'll give you a clue/hint.

我会给你一些提示。

You can do it this way.

你可以这样来做。

Take notes, please.

请做笔记。

Are you clear?

明白了吗?

Is that right/correct?

那个正确吗?

Can you find the mistakes?

你能找出错误吗?

Do you know how to correct the mistakes?

你知道怎么改错吗?

Are you ready?

准备好了吗?

Can you guess it?

能猜猜吗?

Yes, you're right.

对, 你对了。

I'm sorry. Can you say that again?

对不起。能再说一遍吗?

Take your time.

慢慢来。

Use your head.

动动你的脑筋。

Good idea! That makes sense.

好主意! 有道理。

Watch me and I'll show you.

看着我, 我来演示。

I want all of you to answer this question.

我请大家一起来回答这个问题。

That's all for the new lesson.

新课就到这儿。

That's all for the revision.

复习就到这儿。

I want you to work in pairs.

我想让大家做两人一组的练习。

I want you to work in groups.

请大家进行小组练习。

Do you have any questions?

你们有问题吗?

Understand?

明白了吗?

Clear?

清楚了吗?

Pardon?

再说一遍好吗?

Can you hear me?

能听见吗?

Can you see it?

你能看到它吗?

Could you see the words on the blackboard?

你能看清黑板上的词吗?

布置练习用语

Here's your homework for today.

这是你们今天的家庭作业。

Hand in your homework tomorrow.

你们的家庭作业明天交。

Please pass the exercise books to the front.

请将练习本递到前面来。

Don't copy others' work.

不要抄别人的作业。

For today's homework...

今天的作业是……

Practise after class./Practise at home.

课后请做练习。

Say it out loud, before you write it down.

写之前，请大声朗读。

Copy/Print/Write each word twice.

每个单词写两遍。

Memorize these sentences.

背诵这些句子。

Learn this text by heart.

背诵课文。

Try to remember these words.

试着背诵这些单词。

Do your homework.

做你们的家庭作业。

Do the next lesson.

做下一课。

学校日常活动用语

You shouldn't have done that.

你不应该那样做。

See you.

再见!

See you (soon/later).

一会儿见。

The summer holiday/vacation comes.

暑假到了。

Wish you a good holiday! Have a good/nice/wonderful time in/during the holiday!

祝你们假期愉快!

Wish you good luck!/Good luck to you!

祝你们好运!

 Good trip to you!/Have a good trip!

祝你们旅途愉快!

Remember to finish your vacation work.

记得完成假期作业。

You must keep a diary and read aloud in the morning.

你必须坚持写日记，早晨大声朗读。

Remember safety first.

记住，安全第一。

Think it over before you act.

做事要三思而后行。

Keep in touch with me.

咱们常联系。

If you come across puzzling questions, you can write them in your letters. Welcome you to my home during the holiday.

如果你们遇到不理解的题，可以写信问。欢迎假期到我家来玩。

See you next term/semester.

下学期见。

Welcome you back to school.

欢迎你们返校。

Glad/Nice to meet you again.

很高兴又见到你们。

How time flies!/How fast time goes by!

时间过得真快呀!

A month passed quickly.

一个月很快过去了。

Did you have a good time in the holiday?

你们假期过得好吗?

Where have you been?

你们都到哪里去了?

Where did you go for the holiday? What have you seen there?

你假期去哪里了? 都看到什么了?

How did you spend your holiday?

你的假期是怎样度过的?

Will/Would you say something about your holiday?

讲一讲你的假期生活好吗?

Tell us the most interesting things you have seen/met.

给我们讲一讲你遇见的最有趣的事。

What rewarding/instructive activities did you attend/take part in?

你参加了哪些有益/意义的活动?

What have you learnt in the holiday?

假期你学到了些什么?

What reward have you gained/got in the vacation?

假期有哪些收获?

New term begins, you should have a new start.

新学期开始了, 你们应该有一个新起色。

You should get your minds back to study.

你们应该收回心来学习了。

Time is money.

一寸光阴一寸金。

You must study hard and make progress every day.

你们一定要好好学习, 天天向上。

You should learn from each other and help each other.

你们应该互相学习, 互相帮助。

You should decide/make up your mind to catch up with others.

你应该下决心迎头赶上。

Great efforts will be rewarded by great progress.

肯付出就会有进步。

No pains, no gains.

没有耕耘, 就没有收获。

I will try/do my best to help you if you like.

如果你愿意, 我会尽力帮助你。

Speak out your mind.

把你的想法说出来。

I'd like to be a true friend of yours.

我愿做你真正的朋友。

I hope from my heart that I would be your true friend.

我真心希望做你们的知心朋友。

Do you have confidence?/Are you full of confidence?

你有信心吗?

I believe you, and I believe in you.

我相信你的话,更信任你们。

I'm sure you'll make a great progress in a month.

我相信一个月后,你会取得很大进步。

This term we have nine subjects: Chinese, English, Politics, History, Geography, Math, Physics, Chemistry and Biology.

这学期我们有九门学科:语文、英语、政治、历史、地理、数学、物理、化学和生物。

We also have some other interesting subjects: Music, Fine Arts, Physical Education, etc.

我们还有其他一些有趣的课程:音乐、美术、体育等。

We have one weekly meeting on Monday afternoon.

周一下午我们有个班会。

The head teacher of our class is Mr. Zhang.

我们的班主任是张老师。

You must be polite and say hi to them when you see the teachers.

见到老师要有礼貌，要问好。

When you come into school, you must speak Putonghua.

一进学校，你就要讲普通话。

This class, I'll promote a monitor, and you may take an election for it.

这节课，我想提拔一名班长，大家可以选举。

Do you understand?/Is it understood?

大家明白吗?

Everyone, you're doing a great job.

大家都干得不错。

Don't cry over spilt milk.

不要过于计较。

Let's give the classroom a good cleaning.

让我们打扫一下教室卫生。

Why don't we clean our classroom first?

先打扫教室吧?

What shall we take care of next?

接下来我们还要干什么?

Take these chairs out of the classroom.

把这些椅子拿出教室。

Take these charts off the wall.

把这些图画从墙上取下来。

Why don't we just straighten up a bit?

我们再收拾一下好吗?

Who's the student（with）wearing glasses?

戴眼镜的那位同学叫什么名字?

Her name is on the tip of my tongue.

我一时记不起她的名字了。

I knocked at the office door many times just now.

我刚才敲了很多次办公室的门。

What's the emergency?

什么急事?

Xiao Zhang is badly ill now, we must send for a doctor at once.

小张正病得厉害, 我们要赶紧送他去看医生。

Is there a doctor in the school?

学校里有医生吗?

Somebody call an ambulance 120.

快打急救电话120。

What's eating you?/What's wrong with you?

你到底怎么不舒服?

The doctor told me to take the cold medicine three times a day.

医生告诉我服用感冒药一天三次。

My classmate Zhang Ming got into a fight yesterday.

我的同学张明昨天打架了。

You are injured.

你受伤了。

Freeze, don't make him to lose too much blood.

别乱来,不要让他失血太多。

Tell him not to worry about it.

告诉他,别为这事着急。

Out of the way./Get out.

离开这里。

I'm just playing around with you/joking around with you, no fooling.

我只是在和你开玩笑。

Your thought isn't really right, please think it again.

你的想法不是很合适,请再想想。

Are you going to make any changes to the plan?

你想改变一下计划吗?

We're thinking of giving up our plan.

我们正在琢磨着放弃我们的计划。

They gave up their holidays in order to fulfill their work plan.

为了实施这个工作计划, 他们放弃了假期。

Where are you going to spend the winter holiday?

你打算寒假去哪儿?

I shall wash/clear up after dinner today.

今天晚饭后, 我要收拾一下。

You'd better not stay up late recently.

你近来最好不要熬夜。

It's good to get up early.

早起对自己有好处。

When/What time did you get up this morning?

今天早晨你几点起床?

Do you like morning exercises?

你喜欢晨练吗?

What kind of activity do you often take part in?

你经常参加什么活动项目?

How do you play basketball? What about football?

你的篮球怎么样呢? 足球呢?

He wants to work in a big company as an engineer when he grows up.

他想长大后在大公司里当一名工程师。

It's very dangerous to throw stones at the window glasses.

用石头扔窗户玻璃, 这很危险。

Are you a pet fan?

你是宠物爱好者吗?

What's your favourite animal?

你最喜欢什么动物?

Do you know how to protect the animal?

你知道怎么保护动物吗?

They admitted the problems between themselves.

他们承认他们两人之间有矛盾。

问候用语

Hi!

你好!

Hello!

你们好!

Good morning/afternoon!

早上/下午好!

Good morning/Good afternoon, class/everyone/boys and girls!

同学们，上午/下午好!

How are you?

你们好吗?

Nice to meet/see you.

很高兴见到你们。

Nice to meet you again./It's nice to see you again.

很高兴再次见到你们!

Happy Children's Day.

儿童节快乐!

Merry Christmas!

圣诞节快乐!

Happy Mid-Autumn Day.

中秋节快乐!

Happy birthday to you!

祝你生日快乐!

Happy New Year!

新年快乐!

Happy Teachers' Day!

教师节快乐!

告别用语

Bye!
再见!

Goodbye!/Bye-bye!
再见!

See you!
再见!

See you tomorrow!
明天见!

See you on Tuesday!
星期二见!

Have a nice weekend!
周末愉快!

Have a nice holiday!
假期愉快!

Have a good time!
祝你们玩得愉快!

Hope to see you again.
希望再次见到你们。

表扬用语

Good! (Better!/Best) !

好! (更好! /最好!)

Right!

正确!

Yes!

是的!

Very good!

非常好!

Great!

太棒了!

Wonderful!

非常精彩!

Excellent!

很棒的!

Great job!

做得不错!

Well done!

做得好!

Cool!

太棒了!

That was great!

非常好!

You are great!

你真棒!

You have done a great job.

你做得非常棒。

He has done a good job.

他做得很好!

You are a wonderful boy/girl.

你是个很棒的男孩/女孩。

You are the winner!

你是获胜者!

Congratulations!

祝贺你!

What a bright idea! Thank you.

好主意! 谢谢!

That's a great answer.

回答得好。

You did a good job!

你做得很好!

We're so proud of you!

我们为你骄傲!

Good job!

做得好!

I'm very pleased with your work.

对你的工作我非常满意。

Smart!/Clever!

聪明!

Perfect!

太好了!

You're very professional.

你很专业。

You are such a smart boy/girl!

你是个聪明的男/女孩!

I couldn't believe my ears!

我简直不敢相信!

批评用语

Stop talking!

不要讲话!

Don't be late again!

下次不要再迟到!

Don't do that again!

不要再那么做了!

I'm sorry you are wrong.

很遗憾, 你错了!

I'm sorry, but that's wrong.

很抱歉, 那是错的!

Who'd like to answer the question?

谁来回答这个问题?

Who can answer the question?

谁能回答这个问题?

Who knows the answer?

谁知道答案?

Who'd like to have a try?

谁来试一下?

Would you like to try, Mary?

玛丽, 你试一下好吗?

Tom, would you like to have a try?

汤姆, 你来试一试?

Do you want to try?

你想试一下吗?

Would you like a second try?

你想再试一下吗?

提问语

Would you like someone to help you?

你想找个人帮你一下吗?

Who'd like to help?

谁能帮一下?

Who'd like to read the text?

谁来读课文?

Who can spell the word "..."?

谁能拼出……这个词?

Can you spell the word "..."?

你能拼出……这个词吗?

Do you know the Chinese/English of the word...?

你知道……这个词的中文/英文吗?

What's the English/Chinese for "..."?

这个词的英文/中文是……?

Any volunteer?

有自愿的吗?

Any one/boy/girl?

有哪个孩子自愿吗?

Have I made it clear?

我说清楚了吗?

Is it clear to you?

你清楚了吗?

You see the point?

你明白了吗?

Got it?/Did you get it?

明白了吗?

Are you OK with the practice?

这个练习合适吗?

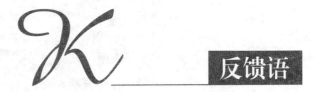

反馈语

Not bad. Thank you. I' m sure you can do better next time.

不错。谢谢! 我相信下次你能做得更好。

Good! Thank you. I could see you' ve practised a lot.

好! 谢谢! 我看得出你练习了很久。

Good boy/girl. That' s a good answer. Thank you.

好孩子。回答得好。谢谢!

Quite good! I really appreciate your effort.

太好了。我很欣赏你的努力。

Great! You did a good job.

好! 你做得好!

Excellent! Let' s give him/her a big hand!

非常好! 让我们为他/她鼓掌。

Wonderful! I' m so proud of you.

很好! 我为你骄傲。

Well done! Good boy/girl.

做得好! 好孩子。

Your answer is very good!

你的回答很好!

I admire your work.

我很佩服你的工作。

Nice doing!

做得好!

You make a great progress.

你进步很快。

II

数学教学案例一
Mathematics Teaching Case One

Getting to Know Ratio

比的认识

一、教学目标　Teaching Aims

1. 使学生理解比的意义。

Enable the students to understand the meaning of ratio.

2. 掌握读写比的方法。

Master the way how to write ratio, and how to read ratio.

3. 理解比、除法、分数之间的关系。

Understand the relationship among ratio, division and fraction.

二、教学难点　Teaching Difficult Points

Understand the relationship among ratio, division and fraction.

理解比、除法、分数之间的关系。

三、教学步骤　Teaching Procedure

步骤一　认识比

师: 这是一面国旗, 如果它的长是3分米、宽是2分米。那么, 宽是长的多少倍? 长是宽的几分之几呢? 谁想试一下?

生: 3除以2等于二分之三

生2: 2除以3等于三分之二

生3: 长是宽的3/2, 宽是长的 2/3。

师: 因此, 我们可以说长比宽是3∶2; 宽比长是2∶3。

Step 1　Getting to Know Ratio

T: Here is a national flag, if its length is 3 dm; its width is 2 dm. How many times of the width is the length? What fraction of the length is the width? Who wants to try?

S1: $3 \div 2 = 3/2$

S2: $2 \div 3 = 2/3$

S3: The length is 3/2 times of the width, the width is 2/3 of the length.

T: In math, we can say: The ratio of length to width is 3∶2[板书]; The ratio of width to length is 2∶3[板书].

步骤二　介绍比的前项、后项和比号

师: 那么, 你们能告诉我3:2和2:3的不同点吗?

生: 是的, 它们是不同的, 2和3的位置不一样。

师: 你说的很正确。在3:2中, 前面的3被称为比的前项, 2是比的后项。中间的冒号是比号。比的后项不能是0。

Step 2　Introduce First Item，Back Item and Colon

T: Therefore, could you tell me the difference between 3 : 2 and 2 : 3?

S: Yes, they are different. The positions of 2 and 3 are different.

T: You are right. In 3 : 2, 3 is called the first item of ratio and 2 refers to the back item of ratio. There is a colon between first item and back item. The back item can't be "o".

步骤三　练习

学习比、除法和分数的关系。把比改为分数形式。

21:100=　　32:15=　　5 to 9 =

Step 3　Practice

Study the relationship among ratio, division and fraction. Change the ratios to fraction form.

步骤四 讨论

比的后项不能是"0"，为什么？

Step 4 Discussion

The back item can't be "o". Why ?

四、**Summary** 总结

今天我们学到了什么呢？
What have we learnt today?

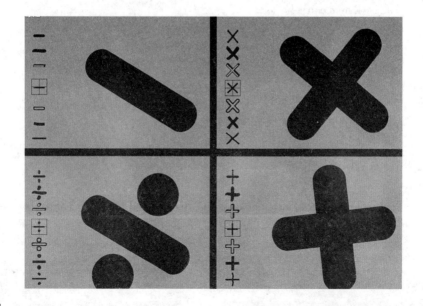

数学教学案例二
Mathematics Teaching Case Two

Numbers from 6 to 10

数字6-10的计算

一、教学目标　Teaching Aims

1. 认识6-10的数字。

To recognize numbers from 6 to 10。

2. 学习加、和、等于、减的定义。

To learn the meanings of plus, and, add, to, is, make, equal, be equal to, minus.

二、教学重点　Teaching Focus

理解加减乘除的含义。

To have a better understanding of add, subtract, multiply and divide.

三、教学步骤　Teaching Procedure

I. 热身　Warrn-up

2+8=?

How much is two plus eight?

加法：5+3=8

Addition: Five plus three is eight.

9−2=?

How much is nine minus two?

减法：7−1=6

Subtraction: Seven minus one is six.

II. 数学中用到的语言　Language You Might Use in Your Math

1. 比一比。Let's compare.

6个苹果 = 6个香蕉。

Six apples equal six bananas.

7 > 6.

Seven is greater than six.

6 <10.

Six is less than ten.

2. 数一数。Let's count.

数一数左数第六个金鱼缸里的鱼。

Count the fish from the left to the sixth goldfish bowl.

里面有几条鱼?

How many fish are there in it ?

哪个金鱼缸里有八条鱼?

Which goldfish bowl has eight fish?

3. 和。Sum.

2 + 4等于6；2和4的和是6。

Two and four is six.

5+ 5等于10；5和5的和是10。

Five and five is ten.

4. 加法。Addition.

2 + 7 = ?

How much is two plus seven?

2 + 7 = 9

Two plus seven is nine.

2 + 7 = 9

Two and seven is equal to nine.

2 + 7 = 9

Two and seven makes nine.

$2 + 7 = 9$

Two added to seven equals nine.

5. 减法。Subtraction.

$9-2＝?$

How much is nine minus two?

$9-2=7$

Nine minus two is seven.

$9-2=7$

Subtract two from nine, you get seven.

6. 连加、连减。Add continuously, subtract continuously.

$5+2+1=8$

Five plus two, plus one is eight.

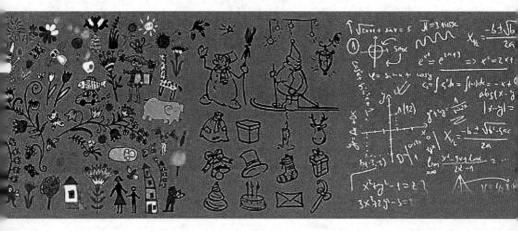

4+2+3=9

Four plus two, plus three is equal to nine.

8–2–2=4

Eight minus two, minus two is four.

7. 加减混合。Mixture of addition and subtraction.

4+3–2=5

Four plus three, minus two is five.

4–2+3=5

Four minus two, plus three is five.

四、Summary 总结

今天你们学到了什么？

What have you learnt today?

Fractions

分数

一、教学目标　Teaching Aims

这是第二节课。学生们已经大体了解了分数的概念。他们知道如何读写分数。这节课，我们将通过一些教学活动进一步学习分数的概念和意义。

This is the second period. Students have known concepts of fractions generally. They know how to read and write fractions. In this class we will identify concepts of fractions by some teaching activities.

二、教学步骤　Teaching Procedure

I. 热身——唱歌　Warm-up—Sing a Song

课程表: 今天, 我们将有英文数学课。我希望每个人都积极地讲英语, 好吗?

Lesson statement: Today we will have an English math class. I hope everyone speaks English actively, OK?

II. 涂色　Color the Paper

分别用红色、黄色和蓝色彩笔在纸上涂色, 然后用分数表示出不同颜色部分所占的比例。教师先做示范。

学生回答: 我画了三个红色的正方形、四个黄色的正方形和两个蓝色正方形。红色的占到3/9, 黄色的占到4/9, 蓝色的占到 2/9。

Color the piece of paper and write out fractions using red, yellow and blue to color the piece of paper. Then write fractions to represent the red parts, yellow parts and blue parts. For example... The teacher shows students how to do this.

Students report: I color three squares red, four squares yellow and two squares blue. The red squares are three ninths of the whole. The yellow squares are four ninths of the whole. The blue squares are two ninths of the whole.

Ⅲ. 看图问答　Look at the Picture of Fruit and Tell Fractions

（1）图中一共有多少水果？

How many fruits are there together?

（2）草莓占多少比例？

Can you use a fraction to represent the red strawberriess?

（3）香蕉呢？

Can you use a fraction to represent the blue bananas?

IV. 练习　Practice

（1）将全班分为7个小组，每个小组有8颗糖果。

Divide the whole class into 7 groups, and each group has 8 candies.

（2）学生将使用分数表示出红色的糖果、黄色的糖果、紫色的糖果和绿色的糖果。

The students will create fractions that represent red candies, yellow candies, purple candies and green candies.

（3）当所有的学生完成后，每个学生分得8颗糖果。

After all of the students have finished this, students divide 8 candies equally.

（4）每个同学用分数表示他/她所得到的不同颜色的糖果数量。

Everyone tells a fraction of candies that he/she gets.

The Recognition of Circle

圆的认识

一、导入课题　Lead-in

1. 提问。Questions.

（1）问：我们已经学习了哪些平面图形？

Q: Which level figures have we learned before?

答：长方形、正方形、梯形和三角形。

A: Rectangle, square, trapezium and triangle.

（2）问：这些平面图形有什么共同点？

Q: What do they have in common?

答：这些都是由线段围成的图形。

A: These figures are formed with line segments.

2. 展开想象引入课题。The topic.

（1）问：如果，我们手中有一块小石头，把它扔进水里，你会看见什么现象呢？

Q: If you throw a stone into the water, what can you see?

答：看见水面荡开一圈圈波纹，就像圆一样。

A: We can see some ripples, and they look like circles.

（2）揭示课题：今天我们就来学习一种新的平面图形——圆。

Solve the problem: Today we are going to study a new plane figure—circle.

3. 请对比长方形、正方形、梯形、三角形，你发现圆形与它们有什么不同？

Let's compare the circle with rectangle, square, trapezium, triangle, what difference can you find?

它们都是由线段围成的图形，但圆是由曲线围成的图形。

They are line figures, but a circle is a curved figure.

圆的定义——圆是平面上的一种曲线图形。

The definition of a circle—A circle is a curved figure on a plane.

4. 在我们生活中哪里能看见圆？

What things are circular in our life?

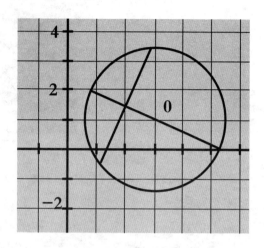

二、探知圆心　The Ascertainment of Centre
[板书]

1. 问: 请同学们看老师或你们自己手中的圆, 有没有什么发现啊?

Q: Look at the circles, what can you find?

答: 没有发现。

A: Nothing.

2. 实践。Practice.

(1) 问: 将手中的圆折一折后, 再观察, 有什么发现呢?

Q: Please fold the circles, now what do you find?

答: 有很多折痕, 而且折出的折痕都相交于圆中心的一点上。

A: There are many creases, and the creases intersect in the centre.

(2) 问: 是不是都一样?

Q: Are they all the same?

答：结果一样。

A：All the same.

3. 给折痕相交的点定一个名字：圆心。

Give the intersect a name: centre.

4. 圆心通常我们用字母"O"来表示。

We use letter "o" to express the centre.

问：请思考一个圆有几个圆心？

Q：Please think about how many centres does a circle have?

答：只有一个。

A：There is only one centre in a circle.

三、探知直径 The Ascertainment of Diameter

1. 实践。Practice.

（1）同学们刚才通过反复对折的方法找到了圆心，那看一下你们的折圆产生的折痕，这些折痕可以看作是我们已经学过的线段，观察有什么发现。

You just found the centre by folding. Now please look at these creases. Do you think they are line segments? What can you see?

所有的折痕都通过圆心。

All the creases go through centre.

两个端点连成线都通过圆心。

The two ends go across the centre of the circle.

（2）问：线段两边的端点呢？

Q: How about the ends?

答：在圆上。

A: On the circle.

2. [出示图] 请看图，指出哪里是圆上。

[*Show the picture*] Please look at this picture, tell us where is on the circle.

3. 小结：通过圆心，并且两个端点都在圆上的线段叫做直径。

Summary: The line is called diameter that goes across the centre and the two ends are on the circle.

我们通常用字母 "d" 来表示直径。

We use letter "d" to express the diameter.

4. 练习：请看图。哪条是直径？为什么？

Pratice: Look. Which one is the diameter? Why?

5. 看这个圆，在同一个圆里会有多少条直径？它们的长度相同吗？

Please look at the circle, how many diameters are there in one circle? Are they the same length?

四、探知半径　The Ascertainment of Radius

1. 请看这个圆，我们知道这样对折的这条通过圆心、两个端点在圆上的线段叫作直径。那这条呢？是不是叫直径？

Look at this circle. We know this line is called diameter as it goes across the centre with the two ends on the circle. How about this line? Is it a diameter? Why?

不是。为什么？它只有一个端点在圆上，另一个端点在圆心上。

No. Why? Because it has one end on the circle but the other end at the centre.

一个端点在圆上：半径（另一个端点在圆心）。

One end on the circle: radius （the other end at the centre）.

2. 这些叫半径。

They are called radius.

3. 小结：我们通常用字母"r"来表示。

Summary: We use letter "r" to express radius.

4. 请看图。哪条是半径，为什么？

Look. Which one is radius, and why?

5. 请看圆。在同一个圆里半径有多少条？它们的长度相同吗？

Please look at the circle. How many radiuses are there in one circle? Are they the same length?

五、探知直径、半径关系 The Ascertainment of the Relationship between Diameter and Radius

1. 请看圆，观察半径和直径有什么关系？

Look at the circle. What is the relationship between diameter and radius?

半径是直径的一半，直径是半径的2倍。

The radius is half of the diameter, and the diameter is two times the radius.

2. 谁能用公式来表示？

Who can use formula to express it?

3. 能用刚才的关系来表示吗？

Can we use the above relationship to express it?

不能。

No, we can't.

由此说明必须在同一个圆内。

It means they must in the same circle.

The Sum of Internal Angles

三角形的内角和

一、教学目标　Teaching Aims

1. 复习角的测量。

Review to measure the degrees of an angle.

2. 帮助学生掌握三角形的内角和。

Help the students grasp the sum of internal angles.

3. 培养学生观察、比较和分析的能力。

Cultivate students' abilities of observation, comparison, and analysis.

二、教学重点　Teaching Focus

如何计算三角形的内角和。

How to find the sum of internal angles?

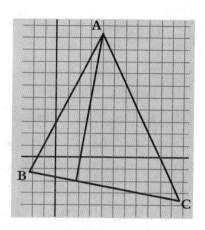

教学资源: 数学课本、练习本、纸条、尺子。

Teaching resource: Mathematics book, exercises books, scrip, ruler.

I. 复习 Revision

1. 请画出三种类型的三角形: 锐角三角形、直角三角形和钝角三角形。

Please draw three kinds of triangles: an acute triangle, a right triangle, an obtuse triangle.

2. 测量每个角的度数, 然后算出内角和。

Please measure the angles of each triangle, then work out the sum of the internal angles.

这三种类型的三角形的内角和一样吗?

Are they same? (three kinds of triangle)

Ⅱ. 新课　A New lesson

1. 做试验。Let's do an experiment.

（1）请画一个直角三角形, 沿着虚线将三角形分为两个三角形。每个三角形的内角和是多少呢?

Please take out one right triangle, cut this triangle along dashed below. What is the sum of internal angles?

（2）再画一个锐角三角形和钝角三角形, 重复上面的做法? 你会有什么发现? 每个三角形的内角和是多少呢?

Please take out one acute triangle and one obtuse triangle, have the same experiments. What can you find? What is the sum of internal angles?

2. 总结。Summary.

三角形的内角和是180。

The sum of internal angles of a triangle is 180.

3. 例子。Example.

在一个三角形中, 如果 $\angle 1=78$, $\angle 2=44$, 那么 $\angle 3=?$

In a triangle, given $\angle 1=78$, $\angle 2=44$, find $\angle 3?$

$\angle 3=180-78-44=58$

4. 练习与讨论。Practice and Discussion.

昆虫

Insects

一、教学目标　Teaching Aims

1. 让学生掌握昆虫的共同特征。

Let the students know the common features of insects.

2. 培养学生的观察能力。

Develop the students' ability of observation.

二、教学重点　Teaching Focus

1. 掌握昆虫的共同特征。

Learn to know some insects and their features.

2. 让学生学会区分昆虫和其他动物。

Improve the students' ability of distinguishing insects from other animals.

三、教学难点　Teaching Difficulty

1. 引导学生仔细观察并总结昆虫的共同特征。

Instruct students to realize the common characters of insects.

2. 提高其表达与观察能力。

Improve the students' expression and develop their ability of observation.

四、教学步骤　Teaching Procedure

I. 导入　Lead-in

（1）以前我们学过许多大的动物，今天我们将学习一些小的动物——昆虫。

We learned a lot of big animals before. Today we are going to learn some small animals. They are insects.

（2）你能说出一些小动物吗？

Can you name any small animals?

（3）为什么蜘蛛不是昆虫，而苍蝇是昆虫？通过今天的学习我们将了解其中的原因。

The spider is not an insect, while the fly is an insect, why? Today we are going to find out the reason.

II. 介绍（新课程） Presentation（New lesson）

1. 找出下列动物的共同特征。

Find out the common features of the following animals.

（1）说出三种动物名称。（蚂蚁、蝴蝶、蜻蜓）

Name 3 animals.（ant, butterfly, dragonfly）

（2）它们有什么共同点?

What are the common features of these animals?

它们的共同特征有: 身体分为三部分。头上有一对触角, 胸部有三对足。

They have 6 legs on the thorax and a pair of feelers on the head. Their bodies can be divided into 3 parts.

（3）观察昆虫标本并找出共同特征。

Observe some insect specimens and tell the common features.

2. 总结昆虫的共同特征。

Summarize the common features of insects.

三种动物属于同一科, 它们都属昆虫类。它们的共同特征有: 身体分为头、胸、腹三部分。头上有一对触角, 胸部有三对足。

The three animals are in the same group. They are called insects. Their common features are that their bodies can be divided into 3 parts—head, thorax and abdomen. There is a pair of feelers on the head, 6 legs on the thorax.

3. 让学生抽签选择问题并与同伴讨论。

Let the students choose some questions and discuss with their partners. Then answer one by one.

（1）说出5种昆虫。

Name 5 insects.

（2）所有昆虫都有翅膀吗？请举例说明。

Do all insects have wings? Please give some examples.

（3）什么昆虫有一对翅膀？什么昆虫有两对翅膀？

What insects have one pair of wings? What insects have two pairs of wings?

（4）什么昆虫的触角长？什么昆虫的触角短？

What insects have long feelers? What insects have short feelers?

（5）什么动物有4个触角？它是昆虫吗？

Which animal has four feelers? Is it an insect?

（6）什么动物有8条腿？它是昆虫吗？

Which animal has eight legs? Is it an insect?

(7)说出昆虫身体的三部分名称。

Name three parts of the body of insect.

(8)昆虫的腿长在什么地方?

Where are the legs of insect?

(9)昆虫的共同特征是什么?

What are the common features of insect?

花的结构

The Structure of Flower

一、教学目标　Teaching Aims

1. 让学生了解花的结构。

Let students know the structure of flower.

2. 培养学生的观察能力。

Develop the student's ability of observation.

二、教学步骤　Teaching Procedure

花是美丽的，所以很多人都喜欢花。但是很少有人能够仔细地观察它们。这节课我们会用放大镜观察花的结构。请大家仔细观察。

Flowers are very beautiful. And many people like them. But people seldom observe them carefully. This class we will observe them with magnifiers. You must do it carefully.

1. 你能举出一些花名吗?

Can you name some flowers?

玫瑰花 rose, 郁金香 tulip, 凤仙花 balsam, 美人蕉 cannas, 百合花 lily , 茉莉花 jasmine, 香豌豆花 sweet pea, 向日葵 sunflower, 牵牛花morning-glory, 金盏花 marigold, 蝴蝶花 iris, 风信花 hyacinth, 黄水仙 daffodil, 菊花 chrysanthemum。

2. 给学生展示一些卷心菜花。花是由几部分组成的呢? 请用放大镜仔细观察, 然后写在黑板上。

Show cabbages with flowers for students. How many parts are made up of the flower? Please observe them with a magnifier. Then draw them on the blackboard.

3. 教授花的各部分的名称。

Teach the names of the parts. Sepal(花萼), petal(花瓣), stamen(雄蕊), pistil(雌蕊).

4. 再次观察, 注意花的每部分的数量。

Observe again and pay attention to the number of each part.

5. 回答问题。Answer questions.

（1）有多少花萼?

How many sepals are there in a flower?

（2）有多少花瓣?

How many petals are there in a flower?

（3）有多少雄蕊?

How many stamens are there in a flower?

（4）有多少雌蕊?

How many pistils are there in a flower?

（5）花萼是什么颜色的?

What color is the sepal?

（6）花瓣是什么颜色的?

What color is the petal?

（7）雄蕊是什么颜色的?

What color is the stamen?

（8）雌蕊是什么颜色的?

What color is the pistil?

6. 向学生展示一朵桃花。请学生指出各部分的名称和数量，并写在书本上。

Show a model of peach flower. Ask the students say the name of each part and write down the number of each part in their books.

温度计

Thermometer

一、教学目标　Teaching Aims

1. 学生应学会温度计的结构和原理。

Let students learn about the structure and principle of the thermometer.

2. 教会学生如何读写温度计显示的读数。

Teach students how to read and write the degrees centigrade.

二、教学重点　Teaching Focus

1. 学习温度计的结构和原理。

Learn about the structure and principle of the thermometer.

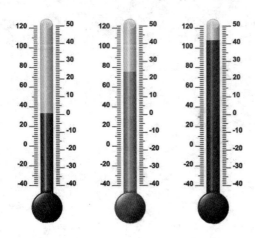

（1）展示温度计并提问。

Show a model of thermometer and ask.

这是什么?

What's it?

（2）温度计的用途是什么?

What is the usage of thermometer?

我们可以使用温度计测量水、空气和人体的温度。

We use the thermometer to measure temperatures of water, air and body.

（3）温度计由几部分组成?

How many parts does the thermometer have?

四部分: 玻璃圈、玻璃管、液泡、红色酒精或者水银。

Four parts—glass ring, glass pipe, glass bubble, red alcohol or azoth.

液泡很细, 所以它很容易破碎。使用时我们应小心。你可以用玻璃圈将温度计挂在墙上。

The glass bubble is very thin. So it is easy to break. We must use it carefully. You can use the glass ring to hang thermometer on the wall.

（4）把温度计放在热水或冷水里，会发生什么现象？

When you put a thermometer into the hot water or cold water, what will happen?

放在热水里，指数会上升；放在冷水里，指数会下降。这就是所谓的热胀冷缩原理。

It rises in hot water and falls in cold water. The principle of the thermometer is that liquid expands with heat and contracts with cold.

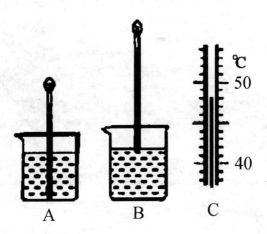

2. 学习读取温度计。

Learn how to read and write the thermometer.

如果温度高于零度, 那么往上数数。如果温度低于零度, 则往下数数。℃ 代表摄氏度。小圆位于C的左上角。

If the temperature is above zero, you count number up. If the temperature is below zero, you count number down. ℃ stand for degree centigrade. The little circle is on the left top of the "C".

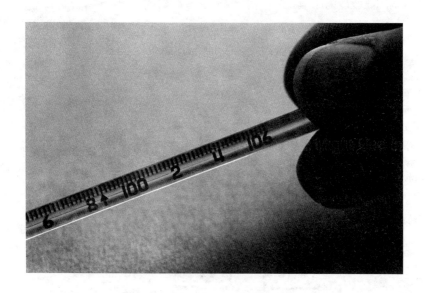

生活中的化学

The Chemical Basis of Life

一、教学目标　Teaching Aims

1. 认识组成生命的化学元素。

To know chemical elements of life constitution.

2. 认识机体中化学元素的重要性。

To know the importance of elements in organisms.

3. 区分生命物质和非生命物质的异同。

To know similarities and differences between living and nonliving matter.

二、教学材料：图片与计算机　Teaching Tools: Picture and Computer

三、教学方法：讨论与总结　Teaching-Means: Discuss and Conclude

四、教学步骤　Teaching Procedure

问题：细胞是什么？细胞是生命物质的最基本的组成成分。我们知道许多生物的大小、形状和组成以及功能都很不同，但是所有生命的基本组成单位却是相似的。所有有生命的物体都是由化学元素组成的。有些元素相同，而有些元素是不同的。通过调查，我们能够了解化学元素的分类、数量和作用。

Question: What is the theory of cell? Cells are the basic structural units of all living things. We know many living things vary in size, shape and composition, and they have different functions, but the basic units of life are quite similar. And all living things have the same chemical basis. Everything is made up of chemical elements. Some have the same, others not the same. By investigating, now we can know the classification, amount and role of these chemical elements.

1. 组成有生命物质的化学元素。

Chemical elements which constitute the living matter.

我们能够从下图得出什么结论？

What can we get from the figure below?

（1）人体中最主要的元素为：碳、氧、氢和氮。

We can know human are mostly made of C, O, H, and N.

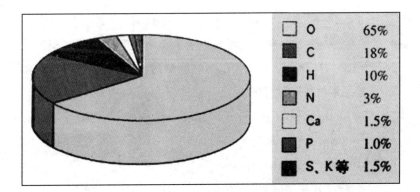

	O	65%
	C	18%
	H	10%
	N	3%
	Ca	1.5%
	P	1.0%
	S、K等	1.5%

（2）人体和动物所含元素类似，但是元素的比例不同。

Human have the same elements, but the amount varies of elements are not the same.

结论：化学元素根据其数量可以分为两种。

Conclusion: chemical elements are divided into 2 classes according to the amount of them.

（1）主要化学元素：比例大于1/10000。

Major elements: in a ratio of more than one in 10, 000.

（2）微量元素：含量很少，但对于人类生命是必需的。

Trace elements: in very small amounts but they are necessary for life.

2. 元素的重要性。

The importance roles of the elements.

（1）所有有生命的物质都含有元素碳。

All living things have a basic element C.

（2）细胞含有6种基本元素，分别是碳、氢、氧、氮、磷和硫。

Cells have 6 basic elements, they are C, H, O, N, P, S.

（3）绝大多数的有机化合物都是由上述几种元素组成的。例如，蛋白质由碳、氢、氧、氮等几种元素组成，核酸由碳、氢、氧、氮、磷组成。这些元素对我们对很重要。

Most of the organic compounds are made up of them. For example, proteins are made of C, H, O, N, and nucleic acids are made of C, H, O, N, and P. They are very important for us.

（4）化学元素影响万物的生长。

Chemical elements influence the growth of living things.

3. 有生命物质和无生命物质的异同。

Similarities and differences between living and nonliving matter.

（1）相同点：所有的元素都存在于有生命物质和无生命物质中。

Similarity: All the elements we can find in living things and nonliving things.

（2）不同点：元素含量是不同的。

Difference: The amounts of elements are different.

探索月球的奥秘

The Moon

一、教学目标　Teaching Aims

1. 让学生了解月球。

Let the students learn about the Moon.

2. 激发学生探索月球的兴趣。

Arouse the students' interest in researching the Moon.

二、教学重点　Teaching Focus

1. 学习月球知识。

Learn about the Moon.

2. 让学生了解月球。

Know the Moon.

3. 能回答一些关于月球的问题。

Can answer some questions about the Moon.

三、教学方法　Teaching Methods

看录像/讨论/游戏/答问题。

Watching the vidio/Discussion/Game/Answering questions.

四、教　具　Teaching Realias

图片/课件/录像。

Pictures/Courseware/Vidio.

五. 教学步骤　Teaching Procedure

I. 问候　Greetings

II. 热身　Warm-up

你喜欢在晚上观察天空吗? 为什么? 宇宙中有许多星球, 其中月球是离地球最近的一颗。今天我们来学习有关月球的知识。

Do you like looking at the sky in the evening? Why? There are many stars in the sky. The Moon is the closest one to the Earth. Today we are going to learn about the Moon.

III. 新课　Presentation

1. 让学生说一说关于月球的知识。/说一说, 你已经知道了哪些关于月球的知识。

Let the kids say something about the Moon. / Please tell me something about the Moon.

2. 关于月球你还有哪些不明白的问题?

Do you have any questions about the Moon?

3. 看录像并思考问题。

Watch the video and think about some questions.

(1)月球有多大?

How big is the Moon?

49个月球等于一个地球。

49 Moons equal an Earth.

(2)月球有多重?

How heavy is the Moon?

81个月球等于一个地球重。

81 Moons equals an earth.

(3)月球的形状是怎样的？

What's the shape of the Moon?

是圆的。

It's round.

(4)月球距离地球有多远？

How far away is it from the Moon to the Earth?

384000千米。

It is 384,000 kms.

(5)月球上的温度怎么样？

How about the temperature on the Moon?

白天很热，晚上很冷。

It's very hot in daytime. But it's very cold at night.

(6)月球上的最高温度是多少？

What is the highest temperature on the Moon?

120摄氏度。

It's 120 degrees.

(7)月球表面有什么？

What's on the surface of the Moon?

一些小山和平原。

Some hills and plains.

(8)月球上一天有多长？

How long is one day on the Moon?

月球上的一天等于地球上的一个月。

One day on the Moon equals one month on the Earth.

（9）A child can lift a big stone on the Moon, why?

为什么一个小孩在月球上能举起一块大石头?

月球的引力很小。

The gravity of the Moon is very small.

（10）1969年发生了什么事?

What happened in 1969?

美国太空飞船到达月球。

American spaceship went to the Moon.

（11）月球上的最低温度是多少？

What is the lowest temperature on the Moon?

零下180度。

180 degrees below zero.

（12）月球能发光吗？为什么？

Can the Moon shine? Why is it bright?

不能。因为它是反射太阳的光。

No, it can't. Because it reflects the rays of the Sun.

（13）月球上有生物吗？为什么？

Are there any living things on the Moon? Why?

没有。因为月球上没有空气和水。

No, there aren't. Because there is no water and air on the Moon.

（14）为什么人在月球上能跳得很高？

Why can a man jump very high on the Moon?

因为月球的引力很小。

Because the gravity of the Moon is very small.

4. 让学生抽签讨论后回答问题。

Send these questions to the students and discuss. Then answer the questions.

IV. 活动　Practice

玩游戏: 传话游戏。

Play a game: Telephone game.

1. 月球上没有空气和水。

There is no water and air on the Moon.

2. 月球的引力很小。

The gravity of the Moon is small.

3. 在月球上你听不到任何声音。

You can't hear any sounds on the Moon.

4. 在月球上你可以跳得很高。

You can jump very high on the Moon.

5. 月球上没有雨。

There is no rain on the Moon.

6. 月球上没有风。

There is no wind on the Moon.

7. 月球不能发光。

The Moon can't shine.

8. 月球上没有树和动物。

There is no trees and animals on the Moon.

9. 月球比太阳小得多。

The Moon is much smaller than the Sun.

V. 小结 Summary

今天我们学了: 大小、距离、天气、重量、引力、生物、光线。

Today we have learned the size, distance, weather, weight, gravity, living things and shine about the moon.

到现在为止, 关于月球还有许多未解之谜。希望我们班将来有人能成为宇航员到月球上去旅行, 探索更多的奥秘。

Up to now, there are many secretes about the Moon, I wish someone in our class will be a spacemen and travel to the Moon and know more about the Moon.

数学专业词汇
Glossary for Mathematics

1. Mathematic Terminologies 数学专业术语

addition	加法	multiplicand	被乘数
subtraction	减法	multiplier	乘数
multiplication	乘法	factor	因数
division	除法	product	积
add	加	dividend	被除数
plus	加	divisor	除数
minus	减	quotient	商
subtract	减	arithmetic	算术
times	乘	mathematics	数学
multiply	乘	geometry	几何
divided by	除	theorem	定理
addend	加数	axiom	公理
sum	和	calculation	计算
minuend	被减数	operation	运算
subtractend	减数	prove	证明
difference	差	hypothesis	假设

proposition	命题	mixed operation	混合运算
greater than	大于	equation	等式
less than	小于	percentage	百分比
equal	等于	the Associative Property	结合律
minimum	最小值	the Distributive Property	分配律
maximum	最大值	the Reflexive Property	交换律
1–digit number	一位数	2 plus 1 equals 3	二加一等于三
2–digit number	两位数	4 minus 2 equals 2	四减二等于二
decimal	小数	4 multiplied by 5, 4 times 5	四乘以五
decimal point	小数点	naught point four	零点四
recurring decimal	循环小数	ratio	比
whole number	整数	proportion	比例
nature number	自然数	numerator	分子
fraction	分数	common denominator	公分母
prime number	质数	unknown	未知数
composite number	合数	equation	等式, 方程式
bar graph	条形统计图	shape	形状
straight line graph	线形统计图	point	点
the Lowest Common	最小公倍数	line	线
the Highest Common	最大公约数	plane	面
average	平均数	solid	体
approximation	近似值	segment	线段
estimation	估算	radial	射线

parallel	平行	circle	圆形
intersect	相交	the center of the circle	圆心
angle	角	ellipse	椭圆
degree	角度	diameter	直径
radian	弧度	triangle	三角形
acute angle	锐角	arc	弧
right angle	直角	semicircle	半圆
obtuse angle	钝角	ring	环
straight angle	平角	circumference	圆周
leg	直角边	right−angled triangle	直角三角形
Pythagorean theorem	勾股定理	acute triangle	锐角三角形
square	正方形	obtuse triangle	钝角三角形
radius	半径	isosceles triangle	等腰三角形
cubic	立方体	point	顶点
rectangle	长方形	equilateral triangle	等边三角形
parallelogram	平行四边形	base angle	底角
trapezium	梯形	line segment	线段
pentagon	五边形	perimeter	周长
hexagon	六边形	length	长
octagon	八边形	width	宽
star	星形	height	高
sector	扇形	side	边（腰）
rhombus	菱形	graph	图表

base	底	pyramid	锥体
cube	立方体	ball	球体
cylinder	圆柱体	vertex	顶角
prism	棱柱	area	面积
circular cone	圆锥体		

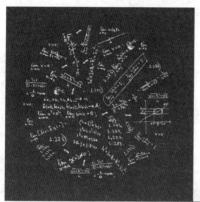

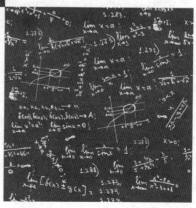

2. Mathematic Signs 数学符号

Sign	符号	《 》French quotes	法文引号; 书名号
. period	句号	¨ tandem colon	双点号
, comma	逗号	″ ditto	同上
: colon	冒号	‖ parallel	双线号
; semicolon	分号	/ virgule	斜线号
! exclamation	惊叹号	& ampersand=and	和
? question mark	问号	~ swung dash	代字号
– hyphen	连字符	§ section; division	分节号
' apostrophe	所有格符号	→ arrow	箭号; 参见号
—dash	破折号	+ plus	加号; 正号
' ' single quotation marks	单引号	— minus	减号; 负号
" " double quotation marks	双引号	± plus or minus	正负号
... ellipsis	省略号	× is multiplied by	乘号
( ) parentheses	圆括号	÷ is divided by	除号
[ ] square brackets	方括号	= is equal to	等于号

≠ is not equal to 不等于号

≡ is equivalent to 全等于号

≌ is equal to or approximately equal to
等于或 约等于号

≈ is approximately equal to 约等于号

< is less than 小于号

> is more than 大于号

≮ is not less than 不小于号

≯ is not more than 不大于号

≤ is less than or equal to 小于等于号

≥ is more than or equal to 大于等于号

% percent 百分之…

‰ permill 千分之…

∞ infinity 无限大号

∝ varies as 与…成比例

√ (square) root 平方根

∷ equals, as (proportion) 等于, 成比例

∵ since; because 因为

∴ hence 所以

∠ angle 角

⌒ semicircle 半圆

⊙ circle 圆

○ circumference 圆周

π pi 圆周率

△ triangle 三角形

⊥ perpendicular to 垂直于

∪ union of 并, 合集

∩ intersection of 交, 通集

∫ the integral of 积分号

Σ (sigma) summation of 总和

° degree 度

′ minute 分

″ second 秒

number 号

℃ Celsius system 摄氏度

@ at 单价

3. Numbers 数

unit (ones) place	个位	ten millions place	千万位
tens place	十位	hundred millions	亿
hundreds place	百位	billions	十亿位
thousands place	千位	tenths place	十分位
ten thousands place	万位	hundredths place	百分位
one hundred thousands place	十万位	thousandths place	千分位
millions place	百万位	ten thousandths place	万分位

4. Reading 数字读法

2.05	two point nought five; two point O five
6.003	six point nought nought three; six point O O three
78.12	seventy–eight point one two
1.5	one point five
2.73	two point seven three
1/3	one third
2/5	two fifths

20%	twenty percent	1/5	one–fifth
75%	seventy–five percent	2/5	two–fifths
100%	one hundred percent	7/8	seven–eighths
0.5%	point five percent	1/10	one–tenth; a tenth
0.46%	point four six percent	3/10	three–tenths
1/2	one–half; a half	1/100	one–hundredth; one percent
1/3	one–third	1/1000	one–thousandth
3/4	three–fourths	1/10000	one ten–thousandth

小学数学与科学分册

XIII

科学专业词汇
Glossary for Science

1. Physical Terminologies　物理专业词汇

absolute error	绝对误差	altimeter	测高仪
absolute motion	绝对运动	ammeter	安培计
absolute temperature	绝对温度	amperemeter	电流计
absolute velocity	绝对速度	ampere	安培
absolute zero	绝对零度	amplitude	振幅
absorption	吸收	angle of rotation	自转角, 转动角
accelerated motion	加速运动	angle of incidence	入射角
acceleration of gravity	重力加速度	angular acceleration	角加速度
acceleration	加速度	angular displacement	角位移
accidental error	偶然误差	angular velocity	角速度
acoustics	声学	anion	负离子
acting force	作用力	annihilation	湮没
adjustment	调节	anode	阳极, 正极
air pump	抽气机	antenna	天线
alternating current (AC)	交流电（路）	applied physics	应用物理学
alternating current generator	交流发电机	Archimedes Principle	阿基米德原理

area	面积	bounce	反弹
argumentation	论证	bound charge	束缚电荷
argument	辐角	bound electron	束缚电子
atomic nucleus	原子核	branch circuit	支路
atomic physics	原子物理学	breakdown	击穿
atomic structure	原子结构	brightness	亮度
atom	原子	Bunsen burner	本生灯
average power	平均功率	buoyancy force	浮力
average velocity	平均速度	camera	照相机
axis of rotation	转动轴	capacitance	电容
balance	天平	capacitor	电容器
barometer	气压计	cathode	阴极
basic quantity	基本量	cell	电池
basic units	基本单位	Celsius scale	摄氏温标
battery charger	电池充电器	centre of gravity	重心
battery accumulator	蓄电池	centre of mass	质心
battery	电池组	centrifugal force	离心力
beam	光束	centripetal acceleration	向心加速度
biconcave	凹凹	centripetal force	向心力
biconvex	凸凸	chain reaction	链式反应
body	物体	chaos	混沌
boiling point	沸点	characteristic spectrum	特征光谱
boiling	沸腾	charged body	带电体

charged particle	带电粒子	conduction	传导
charge	充电，电荷	conduction of heat	热传导
circular motion	圆周运动	conductor	导体
circuit board	电路板	constant force	恒力
classical mechanics	经典力学	constant	常量
classical physics	经典物理学	continuous spectrum	连续谱
coefficient	系数	contraction	收缩
coil	线圈	convergent	全聚的
collision	碰撞	convex	凸
combustible material	可燃物	convex lens	凸透镜
component force	分力	convex mirror	凸面镜
component velocity	分速度	convexo-convex	双凸
composition of forces	力的合成	coordinate system	坐标系
composition of velocities	速度的合成	corpuscular property	粒子性
compression	压缩	corpuscular theory	微粒说
concave	凹	counter	计数器
concave lens	凹透镜	creation	产生
concave mirror	凹面镜	crest	波峰
concavo-concave	双凹	critical angle	临界角
concurrent force	共点力	crystal	晶体
condensation	凝结	current density	电流密度
condenser	电容器	current source	电流源
conducting medium	导电介质	current strength	电流强度

curvilinear motion	曲线运动	driving force	驱动力
cylinder	汽缸, 圆筒	dynamics	动力学
damped vibration	阻尼振动	dry cell	干电池
damping	阻尼	echo	回声
data	数据	eddy current	涡流
data processing	数据处理	effective value	有效值
decay	衰变	elastic body	弹性体
defocusing	散集	elastic force	弹力
density	密度	elasticity	弹性
derived quantity	导出量	electric charge	电荷
derived unit	导出单位	electric circuit	电路
dielectric	电介质	electric current	电流
diffraction	衍射	electric energy	电能
digital timer	数字计时器	electric field	电场
diode	二级管	electric field intensity	电场强度
direct current (DC)	直流	electric field line	电场线
discharge	放电	electric flux	电通量
disorder	无序	electric leakage	漏电
diesel	柴油	electric neutrality	电中性
dispersion	色散	electric potential	电位, 电势
displacement	位移	electric potential difference	电位差, 电势差
divergent	发散的	electric potential energy	电位能
Doppler Effect	多普勒效应	electric power	电功率

electric quantity	电量	electroscope	验电器
electrification	起电	electrostatic induction	静电感应
electrified body	带电体	electrostatic screening	静电屏蔽
electrode	电极	elementary charge	基本电荷, 元电荷
electrolysis	电解	energy	能量
electrolyte	电解质	energy level	能级
electromagnetic induction	电磁感应	equilibrium	平衡
electromagnetic radiation	电磁辐射	equilibrium condition	平衡条件
electromagnetic wave	电磁波	equilibrium of forces	力的平衡
electromagnetic wave spectrum	电磁波谱	equilibrium position	平衡位置
electromagnetism induction phenomenon		equilibrium state	平衡态
	电磁感应现象	equivalent source theorem	等效电源定理
electromagnet	电磁体	error	误差
electromagnetic	电磁的	ether	以太
electrometer	静电计	evaporation	蒸发
electromotive force	电动势	excitation	激发
electron	电子	excitation state	激发态
electron beam	电子束	exert a force	施作用力
electron cloud	电子云	expansion	膨胀
electron microscope	电子显微镜	experiment	实验
electromotive force	电动势	experimental physics	实验物理学
electronegative	电阴性的, 电负性的	external force	外力
electropositive	电阳性的, 电正性的	eyepiece	目镜

far sight	远视	free electron	自由电子
Faraday law of electromagnetic induction		free period	自由周期
	法拉第电磁感应定律	freezing point	凝固点
farad	法拉（电容的单位）	frequency	频率
filament	灯丝	friction	摩擦力
film interference	薄膜干涉	friction force	摩擦力
final velocity	末速度	fusion	聚变
first cosmic velocity	第一宇宙速度	galvanometer	电流计
first law of thermodynamics	热力学第一定律	gas	气体
fission	裂变	general physics	普通物理学
fixed-axis rotation	定轴转动	generator	发电机
flotation balance	浮力秤	good conductor	良导体
fluid	流体	gravitation	引力
fluorescent screen	荧光屏	gravitational potential energy	重力势能
flux	磁通量	gravity	重力
focal length	焦距	gravity field	重力场
focal point	焦点	ground earth	接地
focus	焦点	ground state	基态
focusing	调焦，聚焦	ground wire	地线
force	力	half life period	半衰期
forced vibration	受迫振动	heat	热
fractal	分形	heat capacity	热容
free charge	自由电荷	heat transfer	传热，热传递

heating–insulated vessel	隔热容器	inertial system	惯性系
hertz	赫兹（频率的单位）	infrared ray	红外线
Hooke law	胡克定律	infrared spectrum	红外光谱
humidity	湿度	infrasonic wave	次声波
hydrogen	氢原子	initial phase	初位相
hypothesis	假设	initial velocity	初速度
ice point	冰点	input	输入
ideal gas	理想气体	instantaneous power	瞬时功率
image	像	instantaneous velocity	瞬时速度
image distance	像距	instrument	仪器
image height	像高	internal energy	内能
imaging	成像	insulated conductor	绝缘导体
impulse	冲量	insulating medium	绝缘介质
incident angle	入射角	insulator	绝缘体
incident ray	入射线	intensity	强度
indirect measurement	间接测量	intensity of sound	声强
induced electric current	感应电流	interference	干涉
induced electric field	感应电场	interference fringe	干涉条纹
induction current	感应电流	interference pattern	干涉图样
induction electromotive force	感应电动势	interferometer	干涉仪
induction motor	感应电动机	internal energy	内能
inertia	惯性	internal force	内力
inertial force	惯性力	internal resistance	内阻

intonation	声调		角动量守恒定律
inverted image	倒像	law of conservation of energy	
invisible light	不可见光		能量守恒定律
ion beam	离子束	law of conservation of mass	质量守恒定律
ionization	电离	law of conservation of mechanical energy	
irreversible process	不可逆过程		机械能守恒定律
isobaric process	等压过程	law of conservation of momentum	
isobar	等压线		动量守恒定律
isochoric process	等体积过程	law of electric charge conservation	
isothermal	等温线		电荷守恒定律
isothermal process	等温过程	lead	导线
isotope	同位素	length	长度
Joule	焦耳（功的单位）	lens	透镜
Joule heat	焦耳热	lens formula	透镜公式
Joule law	焦耳定律	light ray	光线
Kepler law	开普勒定律	light source	光源
kinematics	运动学	light wave	光波
kinetic energy	动能	lightning rod	避雷针
kinetics	动力学	light	光
Laplace's Equation	拉普拉斯方程	line spectrum	线状谱
laser	激光，激光器	lines of current	电流线
law	定律	lines of force of electric field	电力线
law of conservation of angular momentum		liquefaction	液化

liquefaction point	液化点	manometer	流体压强计
liquid	液体	mass	质量
longitudinal wave	纵波	mass defect	质量亏损
loop	回路	mass-energy equation	质能方程
luminous intensity	发光强度	matter	物质
magnetic field	磁场	matter wave	物质波
magnetic field intensity	磁场强度	Maxwell's equations	麦克斯韦方程组
magnetic field line	磁场线	mean speed	平均速率
magnetic induction flux	磁感应通量	mean velocity	平均速度
magnetic induction	磁感应强度	measurement	测量
magnetic induction line	磁感应线	mechanical energy	机械能
magnetic material	磁性材料	mechanical motion	机械运动
magnetic needle	磁针	mechanical vibration	机械振动
magnetic pole	磁极	mechanics	力学
magnetics	磁学	medium	介质
magnetism	磁学, 磁性	megawatt	兆瓦
magnetic field	磁场	melting fusion	熔化
magnetic induction	磁感应	melting point	熔点
magnet	磁体, 磁铁	metal calorimeter	金属量热计
magnetization	磁化	meter rule	米尺
magnet	磁体	microdetector	灵敏电流计
magnification	放大率	micrometer caliper	螺旋测微器
magnifier	放大镜, 放大器	microscope	显微镜

microscopic particle	微观粒子	network	网络
mirror reflection	镜面反射	neutralization	中和
mirror	镜	neutron	中子
mixed unit system	混合单位制	newton	牛顿（力的单位）
modern physics	现代物理学	Newton first law	牛顿第一定律
molecular spectrum	分子光谱	Newton second law	牛顿第二定律
molecular structure	分子结构	Newton third law	牛顿第三定律
moment of force	力矩	nonequilibrium state	非平衡态
moment of inertia	转动惯量	nuclear fuel	核燃料
momentum of electromagnetic field		nuclear reaction	核反应
	电磁场的动量	nucleus force	核力
momentum	动量	nucleus of condensation	凝结核
motor	电动机	object	物体
multimeter	多用电表	object distance	物距
musical quality	音色	object height	物高
N pole=North pole	北极	objective	物镜
natural frequency	固有频率	observation	观察
natural light	自然光	Oersted's experiment	奥斯特实验
negative	负	ohm	欧姆
negative charge	负电荷	Ohm law	欧姆定律
negative crystal	负晶体	ohmmeter	欧姆计
negative ion	负离子	Ohm's law	欧姆定律
negative plate	负极板	open circuit	开路

optical centre of lens	透镜光心	peak	峰值
optical fiber	光导纤维	pendulum	摆
optical glass	光学玻璃	penumbra	半影
optical instrument	光学仪器	perfect conductor	理想导体
optical lever	光杠杆	perfect elastic collision	完全弹性碰撞
optical path difference	光程差	perfect inelastic collision	完全非弹性碰撞
optical path	光程（路）	periodicity	周期性
optically denser medium	光密介质	period	周期
optically thinner medium	光疏介质	periscope	潜望镜
optics	光学	permanent magnet	永磁体
orbit	轨道	permittivity of vacuum	真空介电常数
order	有序	permittivity	电容率
oscillograph	示波器	perpetual motion	永恒运动
output	输出	phase	位相
overweight	超重	phenomenon	现象
parallel connection of condensers		photocurrent	光电流
	电容器的并联	photoelectric cell	光电管
parallelogram rule	平行四边形定律	photoelectric effect	光电效应
parallel–resonance circuit	并联谐振电路	photoelectron	光电子
parameter	参量	photography	照相术
particle	质点，粒子	photon	光子
Pascal law	帕斯卡定律	physical balance	物理天平
path	路程	physical property	物理性质

physical quantity	物理量	principle of constancy of light velocity	
physics	物理学		光速不变原理
piezometer	压强计	prism	棱镜
pitch	音调	projectile	抛体
Planck constant	普朗克常量	projectile motion	抛体运动
plasma	等离子体	projector	投影仪
point charge	点电荷	proton	质子
polarization	偏振	pulley	滑轮
polarized light	偏振光	pulley block	滑轮组
pole	磁极	quantity of heat	热量
polycrystal	多晶体	quantization	量子化
poor conductor	不良导体	quantum	量子
positive	正	quantum mechanics	量子力学
positive charge	正电荷	quantum number	量子数
positive crystal	正晶体	quantum theory	量子论
positive ion	正离子	radar	雷达
positive plate	正极板	radiation	辐射
positron	正电子	radioactive source	放射源
potential energy	势能	radius of gyration	回旋半径
potentiometer	电位差计	random motion	无规则运动
power	功率	range	量程
pressure	压力, 压强	rated voltage	额定电压
primary coil	原线圈	ray	线, 射线

reacting force	反作用力	relativity	相对论
real image	实像	resistance	电阻
real object	实物	resistance box	电阻箱
reasoning	推理	resistivity	电阻率
recoil	反冲	resistor	电阻器
rectilinear motion	直线运动	resolution of force	力的分解
reference frame	参考系, 坐标系	resolution of velocity	速度的分解
reference system	参考系	resonance	共振, 共鸣
reflected angle	反射角	resonant frequency	共振频率
reflected ray	反射线	resultant force	合力
reflection	反射	resultant velocity	合速度
reflection coefficient	反射系数	reversibility of optical path	光路可逆性
reflection law	反射定律	reversible process	可逆过程
reflectivity	反射率	rheostat	变阻器
refracted angle	折射角	right–hand screw rule	右手螺旋定则
refracted ray	折射线	rocker	火箭
refraction law	折射定律	rotating magnetic field	旋转磁场
refraction coefficient	折射系数	rotation	自转, 转动
refractive index	折射率	Rutherford scattering	卢瑟福散射
relative acceleration	相对加速度	S pole=South pole	南极
relative error	相对误差	saturation	饱和
relative motion	相对运动	scalar	标量
relative velocity	相对速度	scalar field	标量场

scanner	扫描器	simple machines	简单机械
screw	螺旋桨	simple pendulum	单摆
second cosmic velocity	第二宇宙速度	specific gravity	比重
selective absorption	选择吸收	single crystal（monocrystal）	单晶体
self-induced electromotive force		single slit diffraction	单缝衍射
	自感电动势	sinusoidal alternating current	简谐交流电
self-inductance	自感	sinusoidal current	正弦式电流
self-induction phenomenon	自感系数	sliding friction	滑动摩擦
semiconductor	半导体	slit	狭缝
semi-transparent film	半透膜	solar cell	太阳能电池
sensitive galvanometer	灵敏电流计	solenoid	螺线管
sensitivity	灵敏度	solid	固体
sensitometer	感光计	solidification	凝固
sensor	传感器	solidifying point	凝固点
series connection of condensers		solid state	固态
	电容器的串联	solution	溶液
series-resonance circuit	串联谐振电路	sonar	声纳
shield	护板	sound	声音
short circuit	短路	sound source	声源
shunt resistor	分流电阻	sound velocity	声速
significant figure	有效数字	sound wave	声波
Simple Harmonic Motion（SHM）	简谐运动	source	电源
simple harmonic wave	简谐波	space	空间

spark discharge	火花放电	stationary state	定态
special relativity	狭义相对论	steady current	恒定电流
specific gravity	比重	steady current source	恒流源
specific heat capacity	比热容	steady voltage source	恒压源
spectacles	眼镜	steam point	汽点
spectral analysis	光谱分析	stiffness	劲度
spectral line	光谱线	stimulated radiation	受激辐射
spectrograph	摄谱仪	stop watch	停表
spectrography	摄谱学	suction pump	真空泵, 抽水机
spectroscopy	光谱学	sublimation	升华
spectrum	光谱	superconductivity	超导电性
speed	速率	superconductive material	超导材料
spherical mirror	球面镜	superconductor	超导体
spontaneous radiation	自发辐射	superposition principle of electric field	
spring balance	弹簧秤		电场强度叠加原理
stability	稳定性	superposition theorem	叠加定律
stabilized current supply	稳流电源	supersaturation	过度饱和
stabilized voltage supply	稳压电源	supersonic speed	超声速
standard atmospheric pressure	标准大气压	supersonic wave	超声波
standard cell	标准电池	supply transformer	电源变压器
standing wave	驻波	surface resistance	表面电阻
static friction	静摩擦	switch	开关
statics	静力学	system of concurrent forces	共点力系

system of particles	质点系	third cosmic velocity	第三宇宙速度
system of units	单位制	three-phase alternating current	
systematic error	系统误差		三相[交变]电流
telescope	望远镜	time	时间
temperature	温度	timer	定时器, 计时器
tension	张力	torque	转矩
the law of gravity	万有引力定律	torsion balance	扭秤
theorem	原理	total reflection	全反射
theorem of kinetic energy	动能定理	trajectory	轨道
theorem of momentum	动量定理	transformer	变压器
theoretical physics	理论物理学	transistor	晶体管
thermal capacity	热容量	transition	跃迁
thermal equilibrium	热平衡	translation	平移
thermal motion	热运动	transmission line	传输线
thermal transmission	传热	transmissivity	透射率
thermodynamic scale (of temperature)		transverse wave	横波
	热力学温标	triboelectrification	摩擦起电
thermodynamic temperature	热力学温度	triode	三极管
thermometer	温度计	trough	波谷
thermometric scale	温标	turbine	涡轮
thermonuclear reaction	热核反应	tuning fork	音叉
thick lens	厚透镜	turbulent flow	湍流
thin lens	薄透镜	ultrasound wave	超声波

ultraviolet ray	紫外线	viewing angle	视角
umbra	本影	viewing field	视场
undulatory property	波动性	virtual image	虚像
uniform dielectric	均匀电介质	virtual object	虚物
uniform motion	匀速运动	virtual value	有效值
unit	单位	visibility	可见度
unit system	单位制	visible light	可见光
universal constant	普适常量	voltage	电压
universal gravitation	万有引力	voltage division circuit	分压电路
universal meter	万用电表	voltaic cell	伏打电池
vacuum tube	真空管	voltmeter	伏特计
vacuum	真空	voltmeter–ammeter method	伏安法
value of amplitude	幅值	volt	伏特
vapor	蒸气	volume	体积
vaporization	汽化	vortex electric fiel	涡旋电场
variable	变量	watt	瓦特
vector	矢量, 向量	wave equation	波动方程
velocity of light	光速	wave theory	波动说
velocity	速度	wavelength	波长
verification	验证	wave–particle dualism	波粒二象性
vernier	游标	wave	波
vernier caliper	游标卡尺	weight	重量
vibration	振动	weightlessness	失重

white light	白光	α–decay	α衰变
work	功	α–particle	α粒子
work function	逸出功	α–ray	α射线
X–ray	X射线	β–decay	β衰变
Young experiment	杨氏实验	β–ray	β射线
zero line	零线	γ–decay	γ衰变
		γ–ray	γ射

2. Chemical Terminologies　化学专业术语

product	化学反应产物	crucible melting pot	坩埚, 大熔炉
flask	烧瓶	pipette	吸液管
apparatus	设备	filter	滤管
matrass	卵形瓶	stirring rod	搅拌棒
litmus	石蕊	element	元素
litmus paper	石蕊试纸	periodic table of elements	元素周期表
graduate	量筒	periodic law of elements	元素周期律
graduated flask	量杯	atomic number	原子序数
reagent	试剂	period	周期
test tube	试管	group	族
burette	滴定管	main group	主族
retort	曲颈瓶	body	物体
still	蒸馏釜	compound	化合物
cupel	烤钵	atom	原子

gram atom	克原子	Iodine (I)	碘
atomic weight	原子量	Iron (Fe)	铁
atomic number	原子数	Lead (Pb)	铅
atomic mass	原子质量	Lithium (Li)	锂
molecule	分子	Magnesium (Mg)	镁
electrolyte	电解质	Manganese (Mn)	锰
ion	离子	Mercury (Hg)	汞
element	元素	Molybdenum (Mo)	钼
Aluminium (Al)	铝	Neon (Ne)	氖
Antimony (Sb)	锑	Nickel (Ni)	镍
Bromine (Br)	溴	Nitrogen (N)	氮
Calcium (Ca)	钙	Oxygen (O)	氧
Carbon (C)	碳	Phosphorus (P)	磷
Chlorine (Cl)	氯	Platinum (Pt)	铂
Chromium (Cr)	铬	Polonium (Po)	钋
Cobalt (Co)	钴	Potassium (K)	钾
Copper (Cu)	铜	Radium (Ra)	镭
Fluorine (F)	氟	Radon (Rn)	氡
Gold (Au)	金	Selenium (Se)	硒
Helium (He)	氦	Silicon (Si)	硅
Hydrogen (H)	氢	Silver (Ag)	银

Sodium (Na)	钠	mixture	混合
Sulphur (S)	硫	combination	合成作用
Thallium (Tl)	铊	compound	合成物
Tin (Sn)	锡	alloy	合金
Titanium (Ti)	钛	organic chemistry	有机化学
Tungsten (W)	钨	inorganic chemistry	无机化学
Uranium (U)	铀	derivative	衍生物
Zinc (Zn)	锌	acid	酸
pH indicator	pH值指示剂	hydrochloric acid	盐酸
anion	阴离子	sulphuric acid	硫酸
cation	阳离子	nitric acid	硝酸
electron	电子	aqua fortis	王水
isotope	同位素	fatty acid	脂肪酸
polymer	聚合物	organic acid	有机酸
symbol	复合	alkali	碱, 强碱
radical	基	ammonia	氨
structural formula	分子式	hydrate	水合物
valence, valency	价	hydroxide	氢氧化物
monovalent	单价	hydrocarbon	碳氢化合物
bivalent	二价	alkaloid	生物碱
bond	原子的聚合	aldehyde	醛

oxide	氧化物	hydrolysis	水解
methane	甲烷，沼气	electrolysis	电解
salt	盐	catalyst	催化剂
potassium carbonate	碳酸钾	catalysis	催化作用
soda	苏打	oxidization, oxidation	氧化
sodium carbonate	碳酸钠	reducer	还原剂
analysis	分解	dissolution	分解
fractionation	分馏	synthesis	合成
precipitate	沉淀	protein	蛋白质
distil	蒸馏	ammonia	氨
calcine	煅烧	amino acid	氨基酸
oxidize	氧化	benzene	苯
alkalinization	碱化	superconductive material	超导材料
oxygenate	脱氧，氧化	ozone	臭氧
neutralize	中和	alcohol	醇
hydrogenate	氢化	electrolyte	电解质
dehydrate	脱水	starch	淀粉
fermentation	发酵	nitrogen dioxide	二氧化氮
solution	溶解	sulphur dioxide	二氧化硫
combustion	燃烧	composite	复合材料
fusion, melting	熔解	dry cell	干电池
alkalinity	碱性	glycerol	甘油

polymer	高分子化合物	petroleum	石油
synthetic material	合成材料	plastic	塑料
synthetic fiber	合成纤维	detergent	洗涤剂
synthetic rubber	合成橡胶	cellulose	纤维素
chemical bond	化学键	ethanol	乙醇
chemical equilibrium	化学平衡	ethanal	乙醛
reducing agent	还原剂	ethanoic acid	乙酸
structural formula	结构式	ethene	乙烯
polymerization	聚合反应	oils and fats	油脂
air pollution index	空气污染指数	organic compound	有机化合物
ionic equation	离子方程式	adhesive	黏合剂
lithium cell	锂电池	indicator	指示剂
lead storage battery	铅蓄电池		
fuel cell	燃料电池		
primary battery	原电池		
cracking	裂化		
pyrolysis	裂解		
enzyme	酶		
glucose	葡萄糖		
strong electrolyte	强电解质		
aldehyde	醛		
weak electrolyte	弱电解质		

3. Body 身体词汇

head	头	buttock	屁股
throat	喉咙, 咽喉	skull	颅骨, 头盖骨
armpit hair	腋毛	collarbone	锁骨
nipple	乳头	rib	肋骨
chest	胸部	backbone	脊骨, 脊柱
pit	胸口	shoulder joint	肩关节
navel	肚脐	shoulder blade	肩胛骨
abdomen	腹部	breastbone	胸骨
private parts	阴部	elbow joint	肘关节
thigh	大腿	pelvis	骨盆
neck	脖子	kneecap	膝盖骨
shoulder	肩	bone	骨
back	背	skeleton	骨骼
waist	腰	sinew	腱
hip	臀部	muscle	肌肉

joint	关节	internal organs	内脏
blood vessel	血管	gullet	食管
vein	静脉	stomach	胃
artery	动脉	liver	肝脏
capillary	毛细血管	gall bladder	胆囊
nerve	神经	pancreas	胰腺
spinal marrow	脊髓	spleen	脾
brain	脑	duodenum	十二指肠
respiration	呼吸	small intestine	小肠
windpipe	气管	large intestine	大肠
lung	肺	blind gut	盲肠
heart	心脏	vermiform appendix	阑尾
diaphragm	隔膜	rectum	直肠
exhale	呼出	anus	肛门
inhale	呼入	kidney	肾脏

bladder	膀胱	swallow	咽下
bite	咬	digest	消化
chew	咀嚼	absorb	吸收
knead	揉捏	discharge	排泄
		excrement	粪便

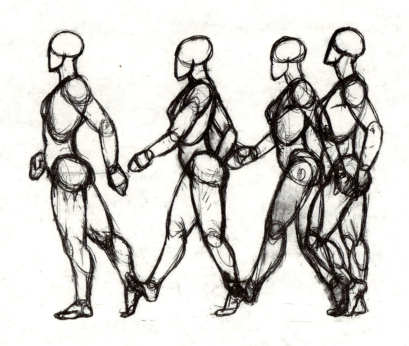

4. Meteorological Terminologies 气象词汇

weather forecast	天气预报	temperate climate	温带气候
weather observation	气象观测	arid climate	干燥气候
weather	天气	tropical monsoon climate	热带季风气候
climate	气候	grassy climate	草原气候
freakish weather	反常天气	desert climate	沙漠气候
muggy weather	闷热天气	coastal climate	沿海气候
continental climate	大陆气候	tropical rainy climate	热带雨林气候
tropical climate	热带气候	marine climate	海洋气候
sub-tropical climate	亚热带气候	tropical marine climate	热带海洋气候
mountain climate	山地气候	littoral climate	海滨气候
winter monsoon climate	冬季季风气候	humid climate	湿润气候
monsoon climate	季风气候	polar climate	极地气候
plateau climate	高原气候	wind scale	风级
highland climate	高地气候	constant wind	恒风
forest climate	森林气候	breeze	微风

headwind	逆风	northeast trades	东北信风
typhoon	台风	hurricane	飓风
calm	无风	southeaster	东南风
light	轻风	typhoon	台风
trade wind	信风	tornado	龙卷风
gentle breeze	微风	gusty wind	疾风
moderate breeze	和风	southwester	西南风
fresh breeze	清风	northwester	西北风
strong breeze	强风	cold front	冷峰
near gale	疾风	favorable wind	顺风
gale	大风	northeaster	东北风
squall	狂风	east wind	东风
strong gale	烈风	north wind	北风
storm	风暴	cyclone	气旋
violent storm	暴风	barometric pressure	气压

high−pressure	高气压	rainy season	雨季
low−pressure	低气压	raindrops	雨点
very rough seas	大浪	heavy rain	大雨
high seas	强浪	light rain	小雨
very high seas	巨浪	intermittent rain	间歇雨
monster waves	狂浪	shower	阵雨
rough seas	中浪	welcome rain	甘霖
moderate seas	小浪	continual rain	断断续续的雨
smooth wavelets	微浪	continuous rain	连续不断的雨
light seas	细浪	downpour	瓢泼大雨
ice	冰	drizzle	毛毛雨
freezing point	冰点	downpour	滂沱大雨
air mass	气团	rainfall	雨量
heat wave	热浪	rainbow	虹
frontal edge	锋面	clear	晴
lightning	闪电	calm	平静
fog	雾	cloudy	多云, 阴天
cool	凉	hail	雹
warm	温暖	thunder	雷
frost	霜	snow	雪
snowdrift	雪堆	snow flake	雪花
dew	露	hot	热
chilly	寒冷	scorching heat	炎热

warm front	暖风	tail	彗尾
eye of a storm	风眼	asteroid	小行星
tidal wave	海啸	aerolite	陨石
landslide	山崩	satellite	卫星
volcanic earthquake	火山地震	constellation	星座
zero	零度	nebula	星云
subzero	零度以下	galaxy	银河
sky	天空	Milky Way	银河
sun	太阳	orbit	轨道
moon	月亮	equator	赤道
star	星星	zenith	天顶
the solar system	太阳系	epicycle	本轮
universal gravitation	万有引力	apogee	远地点
space	太空	perigee	近地点
cosmos	宇宙	node	交点
sphere	天体	limb	边缘
globe	球	light	光
heavenly body	天体	shadow	影子
planet	行星	sound	声音
planetary	行星的	noise	噪音
shooting star	流星	nature	自然
polestar	北极星	water	水
comet	彗星	water cycle	水循环

air	空气	ocean	海洋
earth	地球	natural resources	自然资源
land	陆地	environmental conservation	环境保护

5. Plants 植物

flower	花	marigold	金盏花
seeds	种子	carnation	麝香石竹
rose	玫瑰花	amaryllis	孤挺花
tulip	郁金香	dahlia	大丽花
balsam	凤仙花	pink	石竹花
canna	美人蕉	crocus	番红花
lily	百合花	iris	蝴蝶花
jasmine	茉莉	hyacinth	风信子
sweet pea	香豌豆花	daffodil	黄水仙
sunflower	向日葵	chrysanthemum	菊
geranium	大竺葵	marguerite, daisy	雏菊
morning–glory	牵牛花	gladiolus	剑兰
cosmos	大波斯菊	cantury plant	龙舌兰
pansy	三色堇	magnolia	木兰
poppy	罂粟花	yucca	丝兰

orchid	兰花	daphne	瑞香
freesia	小苍兰	gardenia	栀子
cyclamen	仙客来	lilac	紫丁香
begonia	秋海棠	night-blooming cereus	仙人掌
anemone	银莲花	apple	苹果
wisteria	紫藤	pear	梨
redbud	紫荆	orange	桔子
dogwood	山茱萸	quince	柑橘
hawthorn	山楂	apricot	杏
camellia	山茶	plum	洋李
hydrangea	八仙花	pistil	雌蕊
hibiscus	木槿	ovary	子房
peony	芍药	petal	花瓣
azalea	杜鹃	anther	花药
rhododendron	杜鹃花	stamen	雄蕊

nectar gland	蜜腺	maple	枫树
sepal	萼片	sequoia	红杉
stalk	花柄	fir	冷杉
pollen	花粉	hemlock spruce	铁杉
pine	松	spruce	云杉
cerdar	雪松类	yew	紫杉
larch	落叶松	eucalytus	桉树
juniper	杜松	locust	洋槐
cone	松果	wattle	金合欢树
cypress	柏树	camphor tree	樟树
bamboo	竹	rosewood	紫檀
box	黄杨	ebony	乌檀
laurel	月桂树	sandalwood	檀香木
poplar	白杨	satinwood	椴木
cottonwood	三角叶杨	linden	椴树
osier	紫皮柳树	rowan	欧洲山梨
willow	垂柳	teak	柚木树
birch	白桦	elm	榆木树

oak	橡树	branch	树枝
acorn	橡树果	twig	小树枝
sycamore	美国梧桐	bough	大树枝
ginkgo	银杏树	knot	树节
holly	冬青	trunk	树干
coco	椰树	leaf	树叶
date	枣椰树	sprout	新芽
hickory	山核桃树	sapling	树苗
plane tree	悬铃树	stump	树桩
beech	山毛榉	root	树根
horse chestnut	七叶树	root hair	根毛
blackthorn	黑刺李	taproot	主根
baobab	猴面包树	bark	树皮
elder	接骨木	resin	树脂
myrtle	桃金娘科植物	pith	木髓
cycad	苏铁	cambi	形成层
oil pa	油棕榈树	ring	年轮
treetop	树梢	wood	木材

6. Vegetables 蔬菜

bean	菜豆	horseradish	辣根
cauliflower	菜花	chilli	辣椒
broad bean	蚕豆	asparagus	芦笋
cardoon	刺菜蓟	potato	土豆
scallion	葱	mushroom	蘑菇
rhubarb	大黄	gherkin	嫩黄瓜
watercress	豆瓣菜	parsley	欧芹
French bean	法国菜豆	eggplant	茄子
tomato	番茄	celery	芹菜
pepper	胡椒	garlic	蒜
carrot	胡萝卜	beet	甜菜
cauliflower	花椰菜	melon	甜瓜
cucumber	黄瓜	pimiento	甜椒
leek	韭菜	pea	豌豆
chicory	菊苣	lettuce	莴苣
cabbage	卷心菜	turnip	芜菁

pumpkin	西葫芦	spinach	菠菜
melon	香瓜	leek	韭菜
radish	小萝卜	long crooked squash	菜瓜
chervil	山萝卜, 雪维菜	loofah	丝瓜
onion	洋葱	pumpkin	南瓜
artichoke	洋蓟	bitter gourd	苦瓜
chick–pea	鹰嘴豆	cucumber	黄瓜
brocoli	花椰菜	white gourd	冬瓜
lupin	羽扇豆	gherkin	小黄瓜
cabbage	圆白菜	yam	山芋
kohlrabi	大头菜	taro	芋头
kale	羽衣甘蓝	champignon	香菇
thyme	百里香	needle mushroom	金针菇
fennel	茴香	dried mushroom	冬菇
tarragon	龙嵩	gourd	葫芦
lettuce	生菜		

7. Fruit 水果

pineapple	菠萝	mulberry	桑椹
strawberry	草莓	pomegranate	石榴
guava	番石榴	persimmon	柿子
blood orange	红橙	chestnut	栗子
walnut	胡桃	peach	桃子
peanut	花生	fig	无花果
orange	桔子	watermelon	西瓜
pear	梨	banana	香蕉
plum	李子	apricot	杏
lichee	荔枝	coconut	椰子
mango	芒果		
lemon	柠檬		
loquat	枇杷		
apple	苹果		
grape	葡萄		

8. Seasoning 调味品

caviar	鱼子酱	star anise	八角
barbeque sauce	沙茶酱	cinnamon	肉挂
tomato ketchup/sauce	番茄酱	curry	咖喱
mustard	芥末	maltose	麦芽糖
salt	盐		
sugar	糖		
vinegar	醋		
sweet	甜		
sour	酸		
bitter	苦		
lard	猪油		
peanut oil	花生油		
soy sauce	酱油		
green pepper	青椒		
paprika	红椒		

9. Animals 动物

pet	宠物	goat	山羊
horse	马	lamb	羊羔, 羔羊
mare	母马	zebra	斑马
colt, foal	马驹, 小马	antilope	羚羊
pony	矮马	gazelle	小羚羊
mule	骡	deer	鹿
ass, donkey	驴	reindeer	驯鹿
ox	牛	giraffe	长颈鹿
buffalo	水牛	camel	骆驼
bull	公牛	dromedary	单峰驼
cow	母牛	llama	大羊驼
calf	小牛, 牛犊	guanaco	原驼
pig, swine	猪	alpaca	羊驼
sheep	羊	vicuna	小羊驼
ewe	母羊	elephant	象

rhinoceros	犀牛	otter	水獭
hippopotamus	河马	fox	狐
cat	猫	hyena	鬣狗
kitten, kitty, pussy	小猫	wolf	狼
lion	狮	squirrel	松鼠
lynx	猞猁	dormouse	睡鼠
panther, puma	美洲豹	beaver	河狸
leopard	豹	marmot	土拨鼠
tiger	虎	ferret	雪貂
wildcat	野猫	bear	熊
bison	美洲野牛	rabbit	兔子
yak	牦牛	hare	野兔
dog	狗	rat	鼠
badger	獾	Guinea pig	豚鼠
weasel	鼬, 黄鼠狼	marmot	土拨鼠
		mole	鼹鼠
		mouse	家鼠
		vole	田鼠
		monkey	猴子
		chimpanzee	黑猩猩
		gorilla	大猩猩
		orangutan	猩猩
		gibbon	长臂猿
		sloth	獭猴

anteater	食蚁兽	lizard	蜥蜴
duckbill, platypus	鸭嘴兽	chameleon	变色龙
kangaroo	袋鼠	wall lizard	壁虎
koala	考拉, 树袋熊	crocodile	鳄鱼, 非洲鳄
hedgehog	刺猬	alligator	短吻鳄, 美洲鳄
porcupine	箭猪, 豪猪	turtle	龟
bat	蝙蝠	tortoise	玳瑁
armadillo	犰狳	sea turtle	海龟
whale	鲸	frog	青蛙
dolphin	河豚	bullfrog	牛蛙
porpoise	大西洋鼠海豚	toad	蟾蜍
seal	海豹	poultry	家禽
walrus	海象	cock	公鸡
reptile	爬行动物	rooster	公鸡
snake	蛇	hen	母鸡
adder, viper	蝰蛇	chicken	鸡, 雏鸡
boa	王蛇	chick	小鸡
cobra	眼镜蛇	guinea, fowl	珍珠鸡
copperhead	美洲腹蛇	turkey	火鸡
coral snake	银环蛇	duck	鸭
grass snake	草蛇	mallard	野鸭
python	蟒蛇	teal	小野鸭
rattlesnake	响尾蛇	goose	鹅

gannet	塘鹅		鸡
gander	雄鹅	grouse	松鸡
gosling	幼鹅	partridge	石鸡，鹧鸪
gaggle	鹅	ptarmigan	雷鸟
bird	鸟	quail	鹌鹑
eagle	鹰	ostrich	鸵鸟
bald eagle	白头鹰	stork	鹳
condor	秃鹰	woodcock	山鹬
hawk, falcon	隼	snipe	鹬
heron	苍鹰	gull, seagull	海鸥
golden eagle	鸳	albatross	信天翁
vulture	秃鹫	kingfisher	翠鸟
peacock	孔雀	bird of paradise	极乐鸟，天堂鸟
pelican	鹈鹕		
cormorant	鸬鹚		
swan	天鹅		
cob	雄天鹅		
cygnet	小天鹅		
gander, wild goose	雁		
dove	鸽		
pigeon	野鸽		
turtle dove	斑鸠		
pheasant	雉，野		

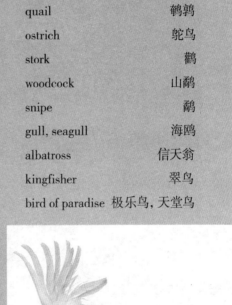

woodpecker	啄木鸟	canary	金丝雀
parrot	鹦鹉	starling	八哥
cockatoo	大葵花鹦鹉	thrush	画眉
macaw	金刚鹦鹉	goldfinch	金翅雀
parakeet	长尾鹦鹉	robin	知更鸟
cuckoo	杜鹃，布谷鸟	swift	褐雨燕
crow	乌鸦	whitethroat	白喉雀
blackbird	乌鸫	hummingbird	蜂雀
magpie	喜鹊	penguin	企鹅
swallow	燕子	owl	猫头鹰
sparrow	麻雀	lark	云雀
nightingale	夜莺		

Postscript 后 记

　　现在呈现在读者面前的这一套教材和读物包括了中小学阶段英语教学的方方面面，主要涵盖四个方面的内容：作为校本教材的中国文化阅读系列，用于英语教师教学技能培训的英语教学理论和实践的专题论著，用于提高英语教师知识和口语能力的教材，还有用于提高其他学科课程教师本专业英语水平的手册。

　　作为编者，我们之所以要编写涉及中小学英语教学如此多方面的内容的系列教材和读物，完全得益于浙江大学外国语言文化与国际交流学院和浙江省宁波市镇海区在2008年开始的一个庞大的共建镇海教育强区的合作项目。镇海区人民政府为了进一步提高本区的外语教育水平，和我院签订了这个长达5年的合作项目，除了教材建设，还有教师培训项目、外语学校合作项目、网络教学项目、民工子弟学校项目等。这些项目为镇海区的外语教育，尤其是英语教育走在全省乃至全国的前列起到了示范作用。

在和镇海区有关领导和同行多次的交流中，我们为教材系列项目制订了一个涉及内容广泛的计划，旨在为镇海中小学教师和学生提供有针对性的支持。由此产生了今天这一整套的教材和读物等书籍的出版。

在系列丛书即将出版之际，我们要向在长达5年的时间里给予我们支持和帮助的有关各方表示衷心的感谢。

首先要感谢的是镇海区人民政府和镇海区教育局，以及镇海中小学教师们的大力支持。正是他们提供的经费支持、教师们的参与以及学生们的配合，保证了这个项目的最终顺利完成。

我们还要感谢浙江大学外国语言文化与国际交流学院的领导、各有关部门的同事和同行的指导和帮助。

作为主持这个项目的负责人，我还要感谢参与这个项目的所有同行和学生们的无私奉献。正是他们不懈的努力和勤奋的工作，使得这个项目得以圆满完成。

黄建滨

2014年1月于求是园

图书在版编目（CIP）数据

双语教师手册.小学数学与科学分册 / 黄建滨主编.
—杭州：浙江大学出版社，2014.4
ISBN 978-7-308-12849-0

Ⅰ.①双…　Ⅱ.①黄…　Ⅲ.①小学数学课–双语教学–
教学参考资料–汉、英②科学知识–小学–双语教学–教学参
考资料–汉、英 Ⅳ.①G623

中国版本图书馆CIP数据核字（2014）第018395号

双　语　教　师　手　册
小学数学与科学分册
黄建滨　主编

丛书策划	张　琛
责任编辑	张颖琪
封面设计	续设计
出版发行	浙江大学出版社
	（杭州市天目山路148号　邮政编码 310007）
	（网址：http://www.zjupress.com）
排　　版	杭州金旭广告有限公司
印　　刷	杭州丰源印刷有限公司
开　　本	880mm × 1230mm　1/32
印　　张	4.75
字　　数	130千
版 印 次	2014年4月第1版　2014年4月第1次印刷
书　　号	ISBN 978-7-308-12849-0
定　　价	18.00元